AF472306

Reflections of Life

A Collection of Poems and Short Stories

Claudia Alston McGregor

ISBN: 978-1-4834-6541-8 (sc)
ISBN: 978-1-4834-6542-5 (e)

Library of Congress Control Number: 2017902125

Lulu Publishing Services rev. date: 03/23/2017

Contents

Introduction ix

A Glimpse of Heaven 1
Mother Is Gone 2
Those Last Precious Miles 3
In Memory of Mother 4
Mother Is Happy Now 5
Dreams of Childhood Days 6
Our Father's Son 7
A Noble Love 8
Only God Made the Seed 9
God's Special Gifts 10
Eternity 11
Golgotha 12
His Hands 14
Life's Highway 15
Morning Prayer 16
Infinite Spirit 17
Light That Leads Home 19
The Search Is Over 20
Lord, Keep Us in Your Hand 21
Here for Just a While 22
Immortality 23
The Master Craftsman 24
Lord, Keep Me from Pride 26
Sundays When I Was Young 27

Loving Pets 28
First Winter Snow 29
Reminiscing 30
The Lonely People 31
South Carolina 32
God's Little Creatures 33
Challenger 34
Autumn 35
Halloween 36
My Boy 37
My Lady Fair 38
Robin 39
The Hummingbird 40
The White House on the Corner 41
Daddy 42
A Learning Experience 43
Autumn Years 44
America 45
Abortion 46
Joe 47
The Frog House 48
Springtime Awakening 49
The Old Homestead 50
Big Mamma 51
Threewitt's Drugstore 52
Lord, What Can We Do? 53
Once They Were Young 54
Don't Live in Another's Shadow 55
Forget Me Not 56
Littleton 57
Yesterday's Serendipity 58
She is Not Dead 59

Thanksgiving 60
Winter 61
God Is with Us 62
Please Don't 63
The Little Things 64
The County Fair 65
Christmas Eve 66
Gentle Spirit 67
Christmas Many Years Ago 68
Thy Will Be Done 69
Christmas 70
He Is Always There 71
Easter 72
The Summer Rain 73
The Big Rock 74
The Christmas Tree 75
It Hurts To Be Lonely 76
The Mountains 77
The Promise Kept By Mama Nell 78
Uncle Toady's 80
Echoes from the Past 83
Threads of Gold 88

Epilogue 95

Introduction

Reflections of Life, are poems and short stories I began writing after my mothers death to help me find peace from my deep sorrow and grief. It never occurred to me to write stories or especially poetry.

One year after I began to write this book, my daughter and I were reunited after twenty two years of separation. She had been told that her mother was dead when her father kidnapped her just after her third birthday. Although I had legal custody, during that time the law would not go across state lines after a parental abduction.

We tried every way we could to locate them, to no avail. The years passed until one day someone gave her an old newspaper clipping of mine and her fathers wedding announcement detailing my mothers address in Florida as the place we would be going after the wedding. She told her father that she planned to call her grandmother and he knew she would learn the truth. He contacted me and I was able to call her and made plans to see each other as soon as possible. Since then I have been able to attend her wedding in California and be with her when my grandson was born.

I dedicate this book in memory of my sister Joanne who was nearly nine when I was born. She stood by me her whole life and this book shares memories of our lives together. Jo encouraged me to keep writing and to share it with others.

So here it is, and to you my dear sweet Sis until we are together again, from Claudia with loads of Love.

A Glimpse of Heaven

Amid gossamer clouds and angel wings, Mother quietly slipped away
to a city beyond the glistening stars, a place where there's only day.
The beauty was beyond compare. When she reached the heavenly throng,
garlands of flowers were everywhere, and they welcomed her with song.
Then from the crowd she heard a voice, soft and crystal clear.
She looked around, and there Daddy was, calling, "Reenie, I'm over here!"
I can see them now, walking arm in arm without a care or sorrow.
Beside them walk their two boys in a land where there's always tomorrow.

Mother Is Gone

"Mother is gone." They were words I had dreaded for years.
I didn't want to believe that they were true,
but with resignation, dissolved into tears.
Suddenly the world seemed empty, and I felt lost and alone.
She was no longer a part of the earth; it was a hurt that I'd never known.
For a while, I wanted to be a child again; perhaps
Mama would soothe the pain.
Then a voice from the past said, "You're a big girl now."
And I knew she never could again.
We go through many stages when we lose the ones we love,
but with bittersweet reluctance, we say good-bye
and release them to God above.

Those Last Precious Miles

Those last precious miles I will cherish all my days.
The time we took Mother home to rest beneath the clay,
All we had left were her ashes. They traveled with my sister many miles,
but during the last few, they rode on my lap just as she held me as a child.
Her ashes were in a marble casket; only on my heart was a heavy load
when I thought of all the times she'd held me as we traveled this same road.
This sweet burden I was holding carried me nine months beneath her breast.
This little casket held something priceless—my mother on the way to her rest.

In Memory of Mother

In a little marble casket, sitting on a wooden stand,
was all that remained of my mother; she had gone to a better land.
Beside it sat a picture of the mother we used to know,
but it has been many years since her blue eyes had that glow.
Her hair had turned to silver instead of the golden curls we knew;
age had taken the luster from those beautiful eyes of blue.
With tearful hearts we said good-bye and slowly walked away
from the person we called Mother at the place where our loved ones lay.
Someday we will be together again in a land so wondrous and fair.
Again we will see those eyes of blue and beautiful golden hair.

Mother Is Happy Now

She had so little pleasure in the last years of her life.
Her sweet old face was wrinkled with sorrow and with strife.
Anything anyone did for her caused her eyes to fill with tears.
Her heart was filled with happiness; she knew little of her last years.
Now she walks those golden streets with her loved ones that went before.
She's happier than she has ever been; tears and sorrow are no more.

Dreams of Childhood Days

Mornings my mother would rock me and hold me to her breast.
About her was the aroma of bacon and coffee.
These are the memories I love the best.
Oh, those childhood days, how we hate to let them go.
The feeling of warmth and security, when we're older—we miss it so.
I long just to be a child again, if only for a little while,
to have her take me in her arms and see her warm, sweet smile.
But these are merely empty dreams, because Mother has gone away
to a place where all sweet mothers go, a place where little angels play.

Our Father's Son

This is My Son. They nailed Him to a tree.
This is My Son. He died to set you free.
He will live in you, and then you'll be free from sin.
Just walk with Him; He'll give you peace within.

This is My Son. He'll return to earth again.
This is My Son. He will rid the earth of pain.
He is coming soon to take His bride away.
Keep your eyes on Him; you'll not be led astray.

This is My Son. He died at Calvary.
This is My Son. He died that you might see.
He arose again and will live within your heart.
Once he comes in, He never will depart.
Open your heart and invite Him in.
Jesus will deliver you all from sin.

A Noble Love

I am privileged to know someone who willingly went through pain
so her sister could have a baby, giving happiness, her only gain.
I know of no greater love anywhere on this earth
than to hand your sister a baby after you just gave it birth.
We honor people for greatness; their nobility is well known.
But her reward will come when she stands before God's throne.

Only God Made the Seed

We get some seed, till, and sow,
but only God can make them grow.

We do our best work and toil,
but only God can bless the soil.

We read books on gardening, but that's all in vain,
for only God can make it rain.

We use scientific methods relieved of doubts,
but only God controls the droughts.

We can commit it to Him and stop fretting so;
then only God will make them grow.

God's Special Gifts

Thank You, Father, for the special gifts you gave,
like the flowers, trees, and songbirds that help to brighten our days.

Thank You for the moon and stars, hanging in the velvet sky;
You knew we'd need their beauty for our tired and weary eyes.

We are thankful for everything—You have fulfilled our every need—
but thank You most for the special gifts, for on these our spirits feed.

Eternity

There is but a misty veil between life and eternity;
when the veil is rent asunder, our eyes are able to see.

When Jesus comes to claim us, we'll follow in perfect peace.
Joy in His presence is rapturous; the glorious blessings increase.

We'll enter the portals of heaven, drawn by the most brilliant light;
we'll eat of the honey and manna, and drink from the fountain of life.

The songbird's voice is not silenced; it will sing its sweet refrain
as we move through the gardens of glory and walk with our loved ones again.

Golgotha

There upon Golgotha's floor,
the blood-drenched sand used for the shore
when on the cross our Savior died—
one sharp spear thrust through His side.
He made no sound until the glow
of His life's blood ebbed its flow.
Then turning His eyes heavenward, He said,
"Eli, Eli, L'a-ma-sa-bach-tha ni?"
to the One who called Him Son.
He drank the cup; His work was done.
The veil of the temple was rent in twain
when He cried His Father's name, and
then He breathed a humble sigh.
"It is finished," before He died.
The ropes were removed from His nail-pierced hands.
His blood was covered by windswept sand,
and as the storm grew, He was placed in a borrowed tomb,
which He graced for only a few short days.
When he arose, the angels praised.
Later He appeared to those He'd known,
and around His countenance a bright light shown.
Soon it was time for Him to leave
a world that tortures and deceives,

ascending heavenward to His throne,
still in substance, flesh, and bone,
eternally wearing the marks of man
He came to save on His nail-scarred hands.

His Hands

There upon that craggy hill,
our blessed Savior's blood was spilled.
Though spikes were driven through His hands,
they still tenderly beckon the hearts of man—
hands that radiated healing power,
that thwarted death in its final hour;
hands whose touch was gentle and kind,
that soothed all pain and healed the blind;
hands that were clasped in fervent prayer
that His Father's will, His life be spared.
But He already knew this could not be,
so they carried His cross to Calvary.

Life's Highway

As long as I take life's middle road, it seems to be easy and straight,
but when I move closer to God's side, the obstacles get in the way.
We often run into detours on our journeys through this life.
Some lead to a different perspective, while others lead to strife.
After we choose our courses, difficult the road may be,
but when we put God first, our spirits are set free.
The destination is what matters; God will help us if we pray.
If only we ask Him for guidance, He will be glad to show us the way.

Morning Prayer

Father, my night's rest is over, and as I start another day,
if there is someone I can help, Lord, open my eyes. I pray,
"And show me."
Then as I go about my work, taking care of my family task,
if there's someone who needs to talk, I come to you and ask,
"Please tell me."
When I go about my life, if I neglect someone in need
because of being thoughtless, with a shameful heart, I plead,
"Forgive me."

Infinite Spirit

I observe the first pinkish glow of morning on the horizon, and my spirit stirs within me, telling me this is an old familiar friend, infinite as the earth, when God said, "Let there be light," and it was.

When I smell the richness of the earth, I can also taste it, and my spirit tells me this is the substance from which I came and will return once more to become clay, until my soul reclaims it to take form again.

Summer arrives, and the sun brings with it the scent of new-mown hay and a profusion of gardenia blossoms that awaken youthful feelings of enchantment and well-being.

A blackbird alights on a twisted branch nearby, and I see the wisdom of the ages in his eye as he cocks his head to one side to observe me, and it's as if, for one brief moment, our spirits bear witness to secrets as old as time itself.

Twilight turns into night, and the breeze wraps me in a secure blanket of fragrant memories. The pungent scent of sulfur and taste of salt are in the air as waves writhe and churn into shore with the tide, not unlike labor that brings forth life from the water of the womb.

Leaves dance like brightly dressed gypsies when autumn appears, festive and colorful. They rustle as I walk through them, and I am aware of life stirring all around me, preparing for winter, storing provisions, and looking for a safe, dry shelter in which to settle from the cold.

Then winter comes with its crystalline, majestic beauty, and the snow takes little bites of my face and tongue. It swirls around me, inviting me to play in its whiteness. I think as I consider how old Mother Earth is, I am very young by comparison. But, my spirit whispers, She is as infinite as time, for the Ancient of Days has shown me these things through His eyes.

Light That Leads Home

Heavenward—reach! Heavenward, oh glorious light,
lead me heavenward to the wonderful sight
of my loved ones waiting on that far away shore,
to be in God's presence forevermore.
Daddy, dear Daddy, the time has been long
since you held and rocked me and sang lullaby songs,
when you kissed my forehead and tucked me in tight
or sat by my bedside until dawns early light.
Mother, sweet mother, your child is growing old.
There's no comfort or warmth to keep away the cold.
Cradle me close to your bosom and say
the things only a
mother can to take cares away.
Dear Father above, guide this vessel to shore,
and lead me homeward to heaven's bright door.

The Search Is Over

I searched for God far and wide,
never knowing He was by my side.
I looked in churches, large and small;
He was ready to answer, if His name I'd call.
Then I met someone that showed me the way;
all I needed to do was kneel and pray.
I was so blind. Why could I not see?
He was there all the time, just waiting for me.
He stands at your door; you should invite Him in.
He will give you peace and free you of sin.

Lord, Keep Us in Your Hand

Lord, my day's work is over, and it's time for me to rest.
Protect us through the night. Tomorrow help me do my best.
Lord, be with my loved ones. Take them through the day.
Please keep them with You. Have Your angels guide their way.
Lord, be with Your children all across the land.
Show them peace and mercy.
Please, keep them in Your hand.

Here for Just a While

We're here only for a little while,
before we walk the lonesome mile.
We enter the world with our mother's groan,
but when we leave, we go alone.
It's the beginning instead of the end.
We have eternity, and now it begins.
This is so wonderful to look forward to.
There's so much more after life here is through.
When we reach heaven, our loved ones will greet us,
and we'll be with our Savior, because death can't defeat us!

Immortality

My spirit's suspended and floats in the air
As I gaze at my body, still lying there.
My family is together over my lifeless form.
Why must they weep, and why do they mourn?
My friends sent flowers that fill the room
with a heavenly fragrance of the finest perfume.
It is now time for the funeral procession.
The hearse rolls up to take its lifeless possession.
We arrive at the grave. A few words are said.
They turn to leave. Do they know I'm not dead?
One lingers by my grave and begins to weep.
I am not there. I do not sleep!
Now I remember that she cannot hear.
My lonely protest won't reach her ear.
I hear a voice that fills me with love.
My spirit is rising to heaven above!
Everything is so beautiful. There are fountains of water.
I hear a voice saying, "Welcome home, Daughter!"

The Master Craftsman

Most artists are not unlike skilled woodworkers. When woodworkers are ready to carve a masterpiece, they go out and find the most perfect tree—oak, walnut, or cherry—and cull out all of the less desirable, since those are unworthy of the craft. Then they find just the right trees and cut them down, taking only the hearts. They take the rough surfaces and start to chip and shape the wood into finished products.

Then comes the sanding and smoothing of the uneven sides until the woodworkers can feel every imperfection with their fingertips. When the texture feels soft and smooth, like velvet, they begin to seal the wood and rub in the oils that will help preserve it through many years. It is through the artists' sweat, blood, and many sleepless nights of labor that inspiration turns into an obsession that does not let them rest. The end results are beautiful works of art without blemish and are part and parcel of the artists who created them.

All have heard of the carpenter who, instead of looking for only the good, seeks also the imperfect and undesirable. He is able to chip and sand away all imperfections and to smooth in the healing oils until He has made us spotless and without blemish. Unlike other artists, He puts His entirety into His creations, thereby rendering our hearts pure. For these miraculous treasures He paid the ultimate price—His own precious blood!

Understanding that our Savior labored in the very works of His own Father brings the realization that He is ultimately the Master Craftsman.

Lord, Keep Me from Pride

Lord, please make me humble; keep self-righteousness from me.
If I assume I'm better than anyone, please bring me to my knees.
Lord, never let me reach the place where I take my eyes off You
And turn them on your children, finding fault in what they do.
Help me to always remember the sin and pain I faced
Until the day I came to You, and You gave to me Your grace.
Help me to always find good in my fellow man,
remembering they're Your children, and helping them if I can.
Help me to show them Your love, and not in a judgmental way,
for only You have the right to judge; I am to help brighten their day.
Lord, I pray I'll never be guilty of causing anyone to stray,
because I let my foolish pride turn them the other way.

Sundays When I Was Young

Sundays when I was young, we'd get up early in the morning
and walk to Sunday school and church in the small town I was born in.
Tied in mother's fancy handkerchief, I'd have a nickel and dime.
We'd want to stop and play, but Daddy would say, "There's no time."
After church, we'd all go home to see if dinner was done.
Afterward Daddy read us the comics, then we'd ride to visit someone.
Back then, people got together more and without things we have today.
Grownups would just enjoy talking while children would run and play.
Everything is supposed to be better; now there's a lot more that can be done.
But if you never have time to visit, you're missing most of the fun.

Loving Pets

(In memory of Missy)

I think pets are little spirits sent from God above
to help us through our lonely hours and fill our lives with love.
Their love is unconditional, for no matter what we do,
they're always there to welcome us home when
our hard day's work is through.
Their faithful love and companionship we have only for a few short years,
and then they have to leave us with a broken heart and tears.
We must remember the good times, for this is the reason they're here.
They did not come to make us cry, but to fill our lives with cheer.

First Winter Snow

On a cold winter evening, silently it covers all the town.
In a white, dazzling brilliance, its beauty does abound.
The quiet peace and splendor seems sent from God above
To cover the drabness of winter and remind us of His love.
As silently as it came, it slowly disappears,
leaving behind a happy glow we'll remember through the years—
the warm and cozy fireside chats, sharing thoughts with those we know,
hot chocolate, and children playing in the first winter snow.

Reminiscing . . .

Reminiscing about bygone days, our family is together,
sitting around a warm wood stove, never minding the weather,
talking of happy times when we were young with the ones that were so dear.
Christmas, old friends, and lots of food are the times that brought most cheer.
We have memories of ghost stories we used to tell at night,
Then have trouble getting to sleep, 'cause we were petrified with fright.
Everything seemed much better then, but somehow I have my doubts.
There were just as many problems then; they
are just good times to talk about.
Years from now, we'll look back on today with happy thoughts returning.
Remembering all the good times we've had, in
our old hearts, will be a yearning.

The Lonely People

They are unloved and hungry. There's no place to go.
The lonely street people sleep out in the cold.
They are God's children, same as you and me;
they are living beings with human needs.
Once they were babies and were warm and fed.
They had a family and a comfortable bed.
Now they roam the streets, hunt for food in garbage cans,
sleep in boxes, outcast in our land.
If circumstances were different, this could be you and me.
Let's thank God it's not and help those in need.
Dear God, have mercy on these forgotten souls.
They need our love and compassion. Lead them to God's fold.

South Carolina

South Carolina is a beautiful name; it is music to the ear,
like a sweet refrain with golden beaches
and stately mountain views.
The tall pines sway under beautiful skies of blue,
enduring through the Civil War while many brave men died.
They fought a bloody battle; we honor them with pride.
It still has some battle scars to remind us of the past,
But its people are the salt, the preservative
that makes it last.

God's Little Creatures

We have a pet cemetery that's grown through the years,
where we've buried our pets and shed many tears.
There was Iggy the iguana, with colors so bright;
our son took him to kindergarten and gave his teachers a fright.
Joe was our bulldog, a nice friendly fellow.
He looked quite fierce, but he was very mellow.
Then there were Sambo and Pepper, the blackest of cats.
Right alongside them lies Squeaky, our white rat.
We also have our potter's field for every little stray
or animals our cats caught, whose lives we couldn't save.
We can learn from animals' instincts, as natural to them as breath,
their acceptance of God's plan of living, birth, and death.

Challenger

No need to search the ocean deep,
For we're not there; we do not sleep.
When you search, all you will find
are the cast-off earth suits we left behind.
We are no longer bound by earthly chains.
We soar like eagles on angel wings.
We are one with the galaxy; we've reached the stars,
explored the moon, and walked on Mars.
What you say is a tragedy was victory in space.
When Challenger's crew beheld Messiah's face.

Autumn

The beautiful months of autumn have a magnificence all their own:
fields of golden wheat to be harvested, which just months before were sown.
Nature is changing its color scheme, turning leaves, orange, gold, and brown.
Pumpkins are ready for Halloween; the aroma of wood smoke's around.
Animals are getting ready for winter. Frost crystals cover the ground.
Squirrels are busy hiding nuts, hoping they won't be found.
There is something about this season that revives us and renews
When we walk through fields and forests wrapped up in the wonderful view.

Halloween

Jack-o-lantern in windows shining bright
with a menacing smile—what a terrible sight!
Black cats and witches dart here and there.
If you run into one, you'll get quite a scare.
Ghosts and goblins in the darkness of night
lurk in the shadows and keep out of sight.
Bobbing for apples, corn dogs on a stick,
visits to a haunted house, candy apples to lick,
scarecrows in cornfields and jellybeans,
children trick or treating—
that's Halloween.

My Boy

My boy was born in early spring,
when the dogwood blossoms and the songbirds sing.
A bundle from heaven he seemed to be,
but I had my doubts by the time he was three.
His eyes are blue and his skin so fair,
a beautiful boy with platinum hair.
I could write a book about this boy of mine,
of the fun we've had, but there's not enough time.
Memories of wildflowers he brought to me,
animals he'd bring home, his house in the tree,
memories of my boy growing up I'll forever treasure.
And when I'm old and feel alone, I'll back on my life with pleasure.

My Lady Fair

She was born in mid-November, my little Lady Fair,
a cherub of a baby with blue eyes and golden hair.
The days, weeks, and months went by, and she reached the age of one.
Chubby hands reached for everything. She filled my life with sun.
Before I knew what happened, she reached the age of two.
How she loved to dress up and flash those eyes of blue!
Then tragedy struck when she was only three.
That is when my Lady Fair was taken away from me.
I watch when in a crowd to see if she is there.
Would I know her if I saw her?
Does she still have golden hair?
Many years have come and gone, and I'll always remember the day
that her daddy rode into town and stole my Lady Fair away.

Robin

My little Robin
where did you go
with those golden curls?
I loved you so.
You were my angel,
my girl so sweet,
a little lady with
dancing feet.
When I'm in a crowd,
I look for you there.
Would I know you if I saw you.
Do you still have golden hair?
Many years have passed,
but I'll never forget the day
your daddy rode into town
and took my baby girl away.

The Hummingbird

Appearing at my windowsill from I know not where,
this dainty minute creature flits here and there.
Going from flower to flower, jeweled colors, glistening bright—
I watched in fascination; then it disappeared from sight.
Somehow the day was brighter; the world seemed a better place
after seeing this tiny visitor with its lovely elfin grace.
God, in His infinite wisdom, knows when we need a lift,
and when we're most discouraged, He sends beauty as a gift.
Rainbows and hummingbirds are very seldom viewed,
but we're blessed when we see them, and our spirits are renewed.

The White House on the Corner

The white house on the corner
is the house that I was born in.
There was lots of excitement in that place
that cold Sunday morning.
I remember the fun we used to have;
there was hardly a dull day.
Daddy would sit on the porch and rock,
and we'd run in the yard and play.
That old house rang with laughter
in those days long ago.
Christmas, when Santa would come,
was the best time I'll ever know.
Daddy had lots of friends
that would keep us all in stitches,
but I liked Mr. Truett best,
'cause he helped me hide my switches.
If that old house were able to talk,
it could have quite a story to tell.
But I think all it would say is "I wish you were back"
To the ones who loved it so well.

Daddy

He was a very handsome man; this description would be right.
He was a real Southern gentleman in his linen suit of white.
He liked having visitors; his friends would come and stay.
We would all have so much fun, they would hate to go away.
My sister and I adored Daddy; we'd wait for him each night.
He always brought surprises that would fill us with delight.
Daddy was a family man, very strict, but always fair,
not afraid to show his love. We knew how much he cared.
I see him rocking on the porch, when memories come to mind.
He loved living so much, and those were happy times.
He knew how to enjoy life, but he died in his prime,
leaving such an empty place in the life of his girl age nine.

A Learning Experience

Don't be afraid to make mistakes; without them you can't learn.
Just try a little harder, and you should have your turn.
If we never made mistakes, how would we grow?
They should only help us to improve on what we know.
We'll be more understanding and have a lot more care
for others who fail after we've been there.
Don't be afraid to take a chance; success is just around the bend,
and you may find the pot of gold as you reach the rainbow's end.

Autumn Years

It seems our lives are like seasons. Autumn is the last years of our life.
It should be a time of resting and ridding ourselves of strife.
There is gold in the sun awaiting harvest. The
wheat in the field does not toil.
Its accomplishments done for the season, drawing nourishment from the soil.
There's much to learn watching nature and the cycles it goes through.
Like the earth, we have our seasons. Autumn belongs to us too.
The golden years of autumn can be as fruitful as in the past,
as we share our lives with others, making friendships that will last.
When we reach the end of our autumn, then
comes the happiest gathering known;
Like the wheat in the field ripe for harvest, God
will reap the harvest He's sown.

America

We are blessed to live in America,
The land of the brave and the free,
with its beautiful plains and valleys
from its mountains to the sea.
Some people come here from other lands,
and we have varied points of view,
but in common we love America,
and our pride in our country is true.
We have freedom to worship as we believe,
to speak what we have on our mind,
to travel wherever we want to—
a more promising land we'll not find.
Its fertile land and rivers,
and fields rich with amber grain
have nurtured us with abundance.
Its life, coursing through our veins.
We have freedom to pursue our dreams
and the chance to make them come true.
The opportunities it offers are boundless.
Let's revere the red, white, and blue.

Abortion

Remember all the babies
denied their place on earth.
They'll never run through fields of clover,
because their mothers wouldn't give them birth.
They'll never know loving arms
or be held to their mother's breast,
or get in fights with other kids over
whose mom or dad is best.
I'm sure if Jesus is watching,
His eyes are filled with tears
over the precious gifts He gave us
and all those wasted years.

Joe

(In memory of Joseph Albert Smith)

God took some stars from heaven
and sprinkled them in his eyes.
He took a ray of sunshine
and put it in his smile.
The beauty of the earth
He placed within his heart,
and all those who knew him
shared a little part.
This sweet and sensitive spirit,
created by God above,
knew that he was special
but not how he was loved.

The Frog House

When I was just a little girl,
around the age of two,
my sister said, "Make a frog house.
The fairies may leave something for you."

My thoughts pictured beautiful things
as I worked there in the sand:
pearls, diamonds, or maybe rings
to wear on my chubby hands.

Then it was time to take my nap,
and I would go to sleep
with visions of all the pretty things
they would leave for me to keep.

Awake again, my heart full of glee,
I would run out to my frog house
to see what they'd left for me—
a little empty rouge box, a flower, or a bead.

Imagination is life's most precious gems,
and this is the treasure my sister gave to me.
It's something we all need.

Springtime Awakening

Spring is in the air, with gentle breezes blowing.
Somewhere in the distance, I can hear a rooster crowing.
Nature is awakening, and the air is filled with song:
doves cooing, birds singing, and whippoorwills calling all night long.
In the trees and hidden places, creatures begin to build their nests,
making a place to keep their young; there's no time to stop and rest.
In cool emerald-green grasses, buttercups raise their head,
opening their petals to the sun, sparkling yellow in their bed.
Nature is awakening. What a beautiful sight to see!
It must be a little like heaven. What a wonderful place that will be!
Just as in nature's awakening, we'll arrive in a magnificent form.
Like the flowers that seem dead in the winter,
We'll awake in God's kingdom—reborn.

The Old Homestead

The old homestead sits abandoned; once it was lovingly called home.
It used to shelter a family; now it stands there all alone.
It was a welcome sight at the end of a weary day,
with a hot meal waiting in the oven and a bed for a tired body to lay.
Children were happy and played on a swing where the oak tree stands.
The mother worked in the home while the father tilled the land.
It was a warm gathering place after the children were grown
to come and spend the holidays when they had kids of their own.
Gone is the aroma of food cooking on the old wood stove,
the smell of kerosene lamps and of bread rising in loaves.
Now the house is covered in vines; the chimney is falling down;
the porch is splintered and sagging; and there's no one left around.
The place is empty where the farm bell hung; it lies rusting on the ground.
Once it was heard for miles; now the silence has a deafening sound.
Don't feel sad about this old house; it is proud—though worn, it's true.
The warmth and love this house gave
touched many lives before it was through.

Big Mamma

We called her Big Mamma, though she was very small,
a dainty little woman, not even five feet tall.
It was a joy to visit her and see her smiling face
when she gave me candy she kept in a secret place.
She loved to read the Bible while I lay by her side.
She'd read the verses to me and make them come alive!
She could talk for hours of how life used to be;
I'd never tire of listening to the stories she told me.
She would tell about a bear that followed them a while
as they rode in the buggy when she was just a child.
They threw out the baby clothes, and that saved the day,
for when the bear stopped to sniff them, they had time to get away.
Grandmothers are wonderful, and I don't think they know
how much they shape our lives and how their knowledge helps us grow.
She's been gone for many years, but fond memories remain,
and the ideals that were Big Mama,
I'll strive to make live again.

Threewitt's Drugstore

Threewitt's was a drug store the men hung around
to catch up on the news in our little town.
They gathered out front and passed the time of day,
laughing and talking—then went on their way.
These were the good times; life was simpler then.
People took more time to visit with friends.
The old men told stories, reminiscing of days gone by,
as they took a chew of tobacco with a twinkle in their eye.
Threewitt's is closed now; the store out front is bare.
With sadness I remember my daddy's visits there.
I imagine that up in heaven there's a spot with a pretty view,
where Daddy and his friends can gather, and catch up on the news.

Lord, What Can We Do?

Lord, give us wisdom and peace from above.
Help us to know Your will and to walk in Your love.
Please give us strength as our burdens we bear.
Also help us to have faith and know that You care.
Lord, help us to accomplish what You want us to do.
You have given so much to us. What can we do for You?

Once They Were Young

Life becomes burdensome as people grow old.
They live in the past as the memories unfold.
They remember the times when they were young,
the places they've been and the songs they have sung,
When their lives had purpose and everything was right
as they rocked their babies in the middle of the night.
When they raised their family, life had few cares.
They were vital and strong and could go anywhere.
Now all that is past, and they sit and stare,
dreaming of happier times as they rock in their chair.

Don't Live in Another's Shadow

Don't live in anyone's shadow. This, God would not have us do.
He has made us each for a purpose, and our own talents
He expects us to use.
Or one day we may discover, when we look and the shadow is gone,
there is nothing left for cover; we'll be left feeling lost and alone.
Trust only in God for guidance, and use the talents He's given you.
Keep His Word in your heart for a road map;
He will lead you on the path that is true.

Forget Me Not

When I die, one thing I pray:
I've helped someone along life's way.
When in memory, my name is called,
on their face, a smile shall fall.
There'll be sunshine instead of tears
and happy thoughts of fruitful years.
A treasured place within their heart
is reserved for me and won't depart.

Littleton

Littleton, the place of my birth,
the place we spent our happiest years,
is the best little town on earth.
Nearly forty years have gone by
since we had to move away
and left behind the fondest dreams,
when they buried Daddy 'neath the clay.
Last week we returned to Littleton,
the beautiful town of my birth.
This time we brought Mother home
to lay beneath the earth.
Someday, I will return to Littleton,
not for a visit as in the past.
The epitaph should read on my gravestone,
"She is finally home at last."

Yesterday's Serendipity

It seems this old house that was once a home is more lonesome every day,
since the ones that brought the sun inside have grown and moved away.

Reflections of their childhood in my memory do abound,
little treasures lovingly tucked away, forgotten and then found.
But some of the images are cloudy, like the mirror's lost its shine.
They dissolve into vapor too quickly in this attic called my mind

She is Not Dead

She is not dead. Her body is gone,
but her spirit's alive, and her soul lingers on.
When a breeze is blowing and we feel the air,
though we can't see it, it is still there.
Her spirit has moved on to a higher plane,
but she left me a part that will always remain.
When I hear a laugh that sounds like a bell,
I think of that voice I remember so well.
She's among the flowers, and the breeze gentle flows,
dewdrops of morning and a daybreak's first glow.
She drifts with the snow and light misty rain.
Her life had meaning; she lived not in vain.

Thanksgiving

Early Thanksgiving morning, our mother was always awake,
cooking the turkey and dressing, and pies, yams, and cakes.
A delightful aroma filled the house as spicy mincemeat baked.
Appetites longed to be satisfied, and our family could hardly wait.
We gathered around the table, feeling happy and so content
as we gave thanks to God for the feast and blessings He had sent.
When I think back over the years of the pleasant times we had
as I prepare our Thanksgiving meal, I sure miss Mother and Dad.
Now we have our own families, and the tradition we repeat.
As our family sits around the table, the happiest memories we'll keep.

Winter

Winter is the time of year most people don't favor,
but it's my favorite time, and it's memories I savor.
It's a time to just cozy in and sit back and let go,
enjoy playing games together and walking in the snow.
It is a festive season; of the feast we never tire,
roasting marshmallows and popping corn in front of the fire.
We have more time to meditate and understand ourselves,
time to relax with a few good books, dusty from waiting on shelves.
I think winter is a perfect time, more so than the rest of the year,
for us to slow down and get together with ones we hold dear.

God Is with Us

God's presence is visible in so many ways
in things we take for granted and see every day.
Take time to smell a flower, then study its delicate core;
the beauty you will find just cannot be ignored.
Go outside on a winter's night and gaze at the stars above,
glistening in the dark velvet sky; you'll see the scope of His love.
When you are on the seashore, find some sand dollars and shells;
notice the perfection and colors. They have a story to tell.
Hold a newborn baby; look at the tiny hands and feet.
And you'll see God's perfect work in one so little and sweet.
Our Father's given everything to assure us of His love.
Let's open our eyes and see the wonders from God above!

Please Don't

Please don't take your life. Don't you know God loves you?
He put us here for a purpose, and He has things for us to do.
There was a time long ago I felt the same as you.
Life had lost all meaning, but God brought me through.
I thank Him every day for caring so much for me.
He saw in me something that I was unable to see.
Now I find living beautiful; I enjoy each and every day.
And I have Jesus beside me, helping me along the way.
I understand what you're feeling, but your life can be beautiful too.
Just put yourself in God's hands, and He'll do the same for you.

The Little Things

A little smile, a little care
may make a burden lighter to bear.
A few kind words, a kind embrace
will make a hurt easier to face.
A little visit, a little note
will offer a shut-in a ray of hope.
It's the little thing that means so much.
They give meaning to life and add a special touch.

The County Fair

When there's a slight nip in the air, the fair comes to town
with bright colored lights and sawdust on the ground.
A landscape is suddenly transformed into a magic wonderland,
with music from the carousel and shows at the grandstand.
In large steel buildings, folks are hoping for first prize
for cakes, quilts, and livestock, with an expectant look in their eyes.
Our appetites give in to total abandon at the smell of hot dogs in the air,
and we end up with a stomachache, but it sure is fun—the county fair.

Christmas Eve

On Christmas Eve, when we were young, we had trouble going to sleep
and imagined we heard sleigh bells, but would not dare get up and peek.
We would lie there so exited and almost be afraid to breathe,
because Santa Claus might hear us and pack up his sack and leave.
Sometime during the night, sleep would finally win out,
and we'd dream of reindeer and elves. They were real; we had no doubt.
Then real early in the morning, long before the break of day,
Daddy would call, "Santa has come!" and we'd get up without delay.
The living room was now a fairyland. We imagine Santa's being there
as we spied our stockings and toys, and the scent of fruit filled the air.
I have recalled those happy memories as I relived my childhood dreams
and the magic when Santa visited my son is still there for me it seems.

Gentle Spirit

The Spirit of God is gentle and kind.
The comfort He gives is a very rare find.
He is always there if you need a friend,
Waiting until you're ready to invite Him in.
Once you know Him, you'll not want to let go.
Life will have more meaning; you can't help but grow.
He'll never condemn you, and if you happen to fall,
He'll be there to pick you up, if His name you call.
It seems we as Christians could learn a lesson from Him
and have love and patience, instead of being ready to condemn.

Christmas Many Years Ago

In a faraway land, many years ago,
from the heavens came a very bright glow.
It shown on a stable in the darkness of night
and led wise men and shepherds to a wonderful sight.
There on the straw lay a little child.
His mother beside Him was gentle and mild.
The air around Him was charged with love.
All fell on their knees to worship this gift from above.
At Christmas, we feel His love in the carols we sing
about that Child that came to Earth, our Lord and King of kings!

Thy Will Be Done

My soul is tired of this dark vision,
this sinful body that has been its prison,
but until God calls me home, I'll make use of it
to do His will as He sees fit.

Christmas

Christmas is a time for celebration,
glittering lights, and angel hair,
busy shoppers buying presents,
bundled up against cold air.

Kitchens have inviting aromas
as all kinds of good things bake:
a turkey and dressing in the oven,
also cookies, pies, and cakes.

Families enjoy being together
around the Christmas tree,
exchanging gifts with one another,
relaxing and feeling carefree.

The miraculous thing about Christmas
is the Spirit we feel at that time.
If we kept it all through the year.
then living would be sublime.

He Is Always There

When I feel alone and am in despair,
I look for my Savior and find Him there.
He stands by my side, for He always cares,
and all of my burdens He gladly shares.
When I have a cross, I give it to Him.
He does not mind, for He's used to them.
When I met my Savior, I found a true friend.
He has been with me since I let Him in.
The Savior I speak of is known far and wide.
If you call on Him, He'll stand by your side.

Easter

Our gentle Savior suffered and died
as He hung on a cross with two thieves at His side.
He gave His life so that we may live
and receive forgiveness; there's no more He could give.
He arose from the grave and the stone rolled away;
the grave lost its victory, so we have Easter today.
On Easter, we see the promise of resurrection and are blessed
as the earth awakens to life after a winter's long rest.

The Summer Rain

It sure is nice to see it rain on a hot summer day
and feel the refreshing breeze as it moves along its way.
It's also nice to hear rain gently falling in the night,
lulling us into restful sleep, then gone by morning light.
There's something about the smell of rain as it sinks into the ground,
nourishing fields and flowers, and leaving its fragrance around.

The Big Rock

There was a Big Rock out in the woods
we loved to play on it whenever we could.
Often we would go there on warm summer days
have a picnic lunch, then climb it and play.
It was a large rock with wild flowers all around,
we felt it was our rock and our own spot of ground.
This place was so special, as I recall the scene,
that does now and forever live on in my dreams.

The Christmas Tree

There it stands in all its majesty with bright colored presents around,
all dressed up in regal splendor like a sovereign awaiting her crown.
Just hours before, it was one of many Christmas trees forlorn and alone,
now adorned in all of their grandeur, their wonderful fragrance filling homes
gracing our lives during the Christmas season,
adding warmth and a peace so serene.
But before long Christmas will be over;
then their beauty will live only in our dreams.

It Hurts To Be Lonely

"I'm so lonely," she said as she twisted the lace on her gown.
"Mother, I'm so tired," I told her. "Please go back and lie down."
She was old and like a child, and I had so much to do.
Why couldn't she understand I had my life to live too.
Now she is gone, and I have a lot more time,
but I didn't know what lonely was
until I lost that mother of mine.

The Mountains

What is more breathtaking or pleasing to the eye
than a stately mountain reaching to the sky?
In winter, it's a wonderland, magnificent in radiant white,
with snow-covered trees hanging heavy and ice crystals glistening bright.
In springtime, the snow begins to melt, filling the mountain streams.
The laurel and wildflowers emerge, and in summer it's lush and green.
When autumn arrives in the mountains, the view is the most stunning of all,
covered with a profusion of color. We gaze at the scene, enthralled.
As we stand on the top of a mountain, we feel so much nearer to God.
It's as though we're walking in the steps that Jesus and Moses trod.

The Promise Kept By Mama Nell

Mama Nell was my father's grandmother and the matriarch of the family. She was a dainty little woman, born in the early nineteenth century, back when most people measured strength by character more than brawn. In this regard, Mama Nell was very sturdy.

Since my father's parents died when his brothers and sisters were quite young, Mama Nell became their mainstay and was deeply loved and respected. Shortly after my parents' marriage in 1924, they left Columbia for eastern North Carolina to spend their honeymoon with my father's family. While there, my mother became very devoted to Mama Nell, who was bedridden, but expected to recover at any time.

Just before she returned home, my mother was summoned to Mama Nell's bedroom. Later she said Mama Nell looked like a delicate china doll propped against overstuffed pillows, all but lost in the huge bed. She was wearing a white nightgown and cap, and the gown was trimmed with fine lace at the wrist and high neck.

Mama Nell reached for Mother's hand and placed in it a family heirloom—a beautiful cameo brooch. She promised my mother that as soon as her health improved, she would travel to Columbia for a visit to get acquainted with my mother's family.

Upon returning to Columbia, my mother's father let my parents use a few rooms in the upstairs of their large home as an apartment. Soon my parents were settled and very happy to have finally set up housekeeping in their first home together.

One night, after they had gone to sleep, something awoke my mother. She lay in the bed for a long time, trying to go back to sleep. She finally decided to go to the kitchen for a glass of warm milk. When she passed the staircase, she heard a noise like a stair creak, but she thought nothing of it.

As she started back down the long, dark hall to her bedroom, she had the distinct feeling someone was following close behind her. When she had snuggled back into bed, she felt someone watching her. When she looked up, there in the moonlight she could make out the form of a little woman dressed in a white gown and cap. She thought it was her mother and called to her. There was no answer, so she thought perhaps her mother was sleepwalking.

She reached out to lightly tug her gown to awaken her.

Instead, my mother's hand went right through the milky white form, and she could see it over her hand. She was so frozen with fear that it took a moment to get her voice enough to call my father. When she did call, the form slowly turned and started gliding out the door. When my father awakened, he naturally thought Mother had been dreaming.

The next morning, my mother recounted the whole story to my father and the rest of the family, and they attributed it to a young bride's hysteria or a bad dream.

Later, just as my father was getting ready to pull out of the driveway for work, a boy on a bicycle rode up with a telegram from the Western Union that said Mama Nell had passed away the night before.

True to character, Mama Nell had come for a visit, keeping the promise she'd made to my mother as best she could.

Uncle Toady's

A trip to the farm where Uncle Toady lived was the highlight of our summer. There was always a cold glass of buttermilk in the icebox and yeast rolls rising under flour-sack dish towels in the kitchen.

Uncle Toady was my daddy's brother. He lived out in the country in what is called "The Old Home Place." It was a tobacco farm just outside the small town I was born in. Later my cousins stayed with him and ran things because Toady was bedridden the last years of his life.

They had a daughter about my age, and I enjoyed going out for a visit. This was back in the early forties, and homes outside of town had none of the early conveniences, such as electricity or plumbing. My cousin and I played in the storehouses, where they kept the cotton seed and corn.

I remember the fun we used to have climbing the rafters and jumping down into the cottonseed. When we tired of that, we listened to our echoes in the deep well or caught frogs and dressed them in little clothes that we made for them. The smell of the tobacco barn and smoke houses is something I'll never forget.

Aunt Lena was an old black woman who lived there in her own little cabin. I liked visiting her. She would tell us stories while she rocked in her chair and smoked a corncob pipe. Her house always smelled so good—like pomade, wood smoke, and fresh ironing. There was a stone fireplace that almost covered one whole wall; that is how she heated her small cabin. There was always something good cooking in the pot that hung inside that fireplace.

The days were full of adventure and lessons on the farm—like the time I climbed the apple tree and learned about wasps and how not to fool around with them. I also found out that I was allergic to their stings. But Cousin Lou Ellen made a paste of some soda, put it on the stings, and I survived.

The way we took our bath was to fill a tin tub with well water in the kitchen and get in and wash. Octagon was the popular soap back then. It didn't smell good, but it would really make our hair shine.

The outside bathroom was called a privy. If you didn't feel like walking in the dark at night, you used a chamber jar kept under your bed. Most chamber pots usually had a lid, so we could keep them covered. There wasn't much in the way of toilet paper back then, so pages torn from the Sears catalog were quite useful.

The thing I enjoyed most on the farm was having supper by the light of a kerosene lamp. Lou Ellen baked all of her bread, and we'd sit at a long table in the kitchen that was covered in oilcloth. I would eat so much that I made myself sick. After supper, we'd sit and talk and then take the lanterns with us to our rooms. I remember the tranquil music of rain on the tin roof at night. In the morning, we'd awaken to the sound of roosters crowing and cows mooing out in the pasture.

Little Miles was a young black man that worked on the farm. He had grown up there and was like a member of the family. One time they had a Halloween party, and we dressed up in sheets and thought we were real scary. We went out to the old barn and saw Miles, so we started chasing him through the cornfield. He ran and yelled and acted real frightened. We thought that was lots of fun, but looking back, I think Miles had the most fun of all.

Uncle Toady died back in 1951, and since then Lou Ellen and her husband, Carlton, have had all the conveniences put in. The old place is very pretty, but I can't help but miss the charm of the way things used to be when I was a child.

Echoes from the Past

Around the start of the Second World War, I was born in a small town in North Carolina. Through the eyes of a child, we seemed to live in a world set apart, impervious to the outside world and its problems. The townspeople were like one large family and showed concern for one another.

What I remember most about this time was Sundays with the family. Mother made sure our shoes were polished and every hair in place, then she tied our few coins for the offering in the corner of a pretty handkerchief. Then my sister and I walked to Sunday school and church together. In a town that small, we could walk about every place we needed to go.

After church and lunch at home, Daddy would take us to Threewitt's Drug Store for an ice cream cone. The store looked like a Norman Rockwell painting and was typical of that time, with wrought-iron chairs, round marble tabletops, and red-and-white soda straws.

We would get back in the car, licking our ice cream, making sure not to drip any on our clothes, and head to the country for a long ride. If Daddy decided to stop and visit someone, I would have to endure one of Mother's spit baths to make sure every evidence of ice cream was off my face.

In the early summer, Uncle Edward, Aunt Lillian, and my cousins Jimmy and Bonnie came to North Carolina for a long visit with us. They brought their maid to help with the children, and our grandmother often accompanied them.

We lived on a main avenue that ran down the center of town, and we could see all the way to the highway. My sister, Joanne, and I squealed with excitement when their big black Packard turned the corner and headed down the avenue toward our house.

Summers for the children meant tea parties, hide-and-seek, and catching lightning bugs after dark while adults sat on the porch and talked while sipping mint tea.

I also remember us running down the dirt road to the old country store with a few pennies clutched in our sweaty palms. The threshold was about worn through from so many customers entering and leaving over the years. The smell of flour, chicken feed, and rat poison when we walked in the door was familiar.

Inside there was a potbelly stove that the men congregated around in winter. They would bite off a plug of tobacco, chew, and spit in the direction of a rusty coffee can. They tried to outdo each other telling stories.

It was hard to decide which penny candy was best, so we would pool our pennies and get one big bag of licorice sticks, BB Bats, and jawbreakers. We would run home and flop down on the creek bank and share our bounty, then lie back, staring at the sky through the trees, not saying a word while we savored every bite.

Inside the house, the adults lounged and played checkers or cards, while the servants cooked, cleaned, and watched after us children.

Our Uncle William owned a wholesale grocery company, and Daddy worked with him. He would buy food by the case, and we would always have country hams and kegs of cheese in the pantry. Daddy hated waste, so he made sure everything was utilized. He wanted every visitor to our home to be well fed. Back then, things had to be rationed, and each family member had its own little supply of sugar. If we didn't use it sparingly, we did without until it was time to get another supply.

Other summer memories include chasing the ice wagon—to the disdain of our daddy. We liked to get long slivers of ice to suck on hot summer days, but Daddy thought this was unladylike behavior for his little girls.

We loved making mud pies and a frog house that would not cave in when we eased our feet from the moist sand. The fact is, there was a real art to doing that. Most of all, I liked wading in the creek that ran beside our house.

It seemed that Mother always called me in for a bath when I was having the best time of the day, playing in the dirt. After my bath, she would dress me in one of my fresh pinafores, then powder my face and neck real good so I wouldn't get any "blackbeads." Off we'd go for our afternoon walk. Most of the time we would end up visiting someone along the way.

Early mornings at our house, I can remember hearing the clacking of the lawnmower and the sweet smell of cut grass drifting in through the window along with the sounds of someone pulling a wagon down the sidewalk, yelling, "Black—berries! Butter—beans!"

The winter was just as much fun as summer, because our house was always filled with people. My parents loved to entertain, and it caused quite a stir when I invited my first-grade teacher, a very prim old maid, to one of my daddy's Four Roses parties. I also got into a lot of trouble when she caught me wearing Mother's "Pigeon blood ruby dinner ring" to school one day.

The big house we lived in took on an ethereal glow when it snowed. It would be so warm and full of life inside and look so peaceful outside with large flakes gently falling into thick drifts.

Our school was only one block from the house, and we gladly trudged home for lunch through the snow. I remember the welcoming scent of homemade vegetable soup and corn fritters when we opened the door to go inside. After we got into our snowsuits and galoshes to start back to school, we reached for a hot fried apple pie to eat on the way.

We learned not to go out in the snow and rain without our galoshes, because the soles on our shoes would come loose and start flapping, and the heels would swell and begin to peel up. They were made of pressed cardboard instead of rubber or leather. Everything was scarce because of the war. I ruined a lot of patent-leather Mary Jane shoes before Daddy decided it would be more practical for us all to wear oxfords, even if they were less dressy.

On Christmas Eve, we would go to bed real early so Santa Claus could come. We were so excited that our teeth chattered, and I can still hear the sleigh bells. Before daylight Daddy would call excitedly from downstairs that Santa had come and that we needed to "hurry down." We had the choice of one thing that we really wanted, and that was what we got, along with our stocking.

The stockings were our mother's worn-out nylon hose that we washed out and hung up on Christmas Eve. Christmas morning, they would be stretched to the floor with fruit, nuts, bags and bags of dime-store candy, and a big box of raisins with the seeds and stems still in them. Those are the best raisins I have ever eaten! We made stockings last a long time, because we knew it would be a long time before Christmas came again.

Daddy would cook a big Christmas breakfast, and later friends and family would come by to eat and celebrate with us as they had through all the holidays.

Many years have now passed, and most of the people we knew back then have been long gone, including our daddy and mother, who passed years ago.

Sometimes, in the middle of the night, I awaken, and it seems I can hear echoes from the past—the happy voices of Aunt Lillian playing the piano, Daddy picking the banjo, and children laughing and singing "Ring around the Rosie." But slowly it all fades into a deafening silence.

Those of us who remain have tried to keep the old traditions alive for our families and the generations to come. The cherished memories live on in my sister's and my heart, and we both feel that up in heaven there is a lot of celebrating going on.

Threads of Gold

She sat with her mending in her lap. "Not as easy as it once was," she said to herself. Anyone could plainly see a moth had made a tasty meal of her last good Sunday-go-to-meeting frock. The sun shown through the curtains behind her, and her silver hair, which she wore in one long braid coiled into a ball on the back of her head, seemed to glow in the sunlight. Her spectacles rode low on her nose, and for a woman of her stature, she showed a lot of strength. In the past few years, she had suffered many hardships.

Any more, she seemed to live in the past most of the time, with her lips pursed as she thought about years past and the happy times they used to have. After all, there was much more past than future.

She tried to weave the material with the thread so that it would look like the original fabric. She remembered how she could once pluck and clean a chicken before the fire in the old wood stove got hot enough to cook it. Now those once-nimble fingers were gnarled and stiff.

It was finally becoming apparent that, try as she might, she could not mend the hole, which was beginning to look more like a wad of thread than fabric. With a sigh of resignation, she stuffed the dress back into her sewing basket.

As she sat rocking, she recalled that last Sunday. Sister Bessie had worn a new frock to church. "She really thought she was something. Always did think she was better'n everybody else, but I'll show her!" she hissed through her teeth while remembering her egg money kept in a secret place over the stove. She had seen a pretty bolt of cloth the last time she was at the five-and-dime store, but was immediately filled with remorse for having such petty thoughts.

Just then, there was a knock at the kitchen door, and she set her sewing basket down beside her chair and went to answer it. When she peeked out through the curtains, her spirits lifted, and she felt a warm glow come over her at the sight of her oldest and dearest friend. "Poss, come on inside," she called. "You're a sight for sore eyes! I'm so glad you stopped by to see me. How is Lena doing?"

"Oh, she fair to midlin', I guess. But the rumetism been givin' huh a fit lately," he replied. While he talked on, she looked at the crinkles around his wise brown eyes and noticed how for the last few years his hair had begun to look like snow-white lamb's wool. She tried to remember back when they were children and had so much fun playing together.

He had gotten his nickname because of his fondness for possum. He loved it when he'd trap a possum out in the hen house and get his old hound dog, Bo, to kill it for him. Bo would get the possum by the neck and shake it until its bones rattled. When it was apparently dead, Poss would take it from him and skin and clean it. He felt it was a cause for celebration, because not only had he gotten rid of a pesky varmint, but he also had a fine feast. Poss loved his possum roasted and liked sweet potatoes and collards to go with it plus hoe cake to sop up the gravy.

When her children were young, Poss would whittle small toys for them, such as whistles or toy animals. He and Lena could never have children of their own, but Lena was a good neighbor and always came over to help out if there was sickness or to bring food if there was a death in the family. It was considered disrespectful for children to call adults by their first name, so she taught children to call them Uncle Poss and Aunt Lena.

Then she heard a voice and realized her thoughts had been far away. She reluctantly, began to travel back to the present. All of her own children had grown up and moved away, and her husband had been dead for thirty years. She had always been blessed with a lot of good friends and neighbors.

As the mist cleared from her daydream, she heard Poss saying, “Dees here come otta de missus gardin. She wont me to brot yo sumpin’ good from huh gardin.”

“My goodness, those greens do look good!” she exclaimed. “I will get me some hog jowl to cook in them and make some crackling cornbread and have them tomorrow. Be sure to tell Lena how much I appreciate them.”

About then, Poss decided that he would leave for home. She cut him a large slice of cake with caramel icing that she had sitting on the table; she had caught him staring hungrily at it a few times. She wrapped it in wax paper for him to take home and share with Lena. “Tell Lena to take care and not overdo it,” she said. “I’ll be over to check in on her in the next few days. Oh, by the way, I saved some slop for your hogs. There’s not as much as I used to have, since I don’t have the crowd to cook for anymore. It’s in the lard can over by the stove. Just bring the can back next time you come.”

Poss thanked her profusely and left.

She returned to her chair in the dining room, and her thoughts went to her children. She wondered if they would be able to make it home for the holidays. Most of her grandchildren were grown and had their own families; consequently, some of her children had their own traditional holiday celebration in order to have their family in one place.

It was turning a little nippy, and the leaves were starting to change color. She would soon need to get her provisions together for the long, cold winter months ahead. Since it was a two-block walk to town, it took a while to get everything she needed and took a lot of preparation for a family gathering the size of hers. She felt a thrill of excitement at the thought of having the old house full of joyous laughter and voices again, so she decided that the next day she would begin making plans for her holiday shopping.

After a small bowl of soup and cornbread, she finished her buttermilk and rinsed the dishes before going to bed. Sleep wouldn't come, because she started remembering all the happy Christmas holidays from years past, when her children were young. Her children never got a lot of toys, but they seemed to enjoy Christmas just as much as the grandchildren, who get many. Most of her children's gifts were homemade rag dolls for the girls, and her husband made a wooden rocking horse or wagon, working late at night on them to be sure the boys didn't see them before Christmas morning.

One of the things they were always able to do was provide good food. During the holidays, there was always an abundance of good things to eat. She had eight children in her family, and her welcome mat was always out to the rest of the family as well as neighbors that would like to come by for a celebration.

She started baking her fruitcakes about two weeks before Thanksgiving, and from then on there was an aroma of something good cooking all the time. By Christmas, the sideboard looked like it would collapse under the weight of pies, cakes, cookies, and trays of fudge filled with pecans and other confections. The tremendous turkey occupied the center of the table while every little space that could be found was filled with spiced peaches, apples, pickles, giblet gravy, sweet potato casserole, dressing, corn pudding, and vegetables. There was hardly room to sit and eat! She always baked her own bread and had a special table set up just to handle the overflow and breads. And of course the kitchen still had plenty in reserve in case something ran low.

She would always include the children in decorating and preparations. They strung popcorn and cranberries for the tree and cut out cookies and decorated them with white sugar and rock candy crystals. She kept candied orange rind around for the children, which they loved. When it was cooking on the stove, it gave the house the familiar scent of Christmas. Most fun of all was when they had their friends over for a taffy pull. It was sticky, and it sometimes fell on the floor, but no one seemed to mind when it came time to eat it.

Finally, she drifted off into a peaceful sleep with memories of years past winding in and out of her dreams.

The next day, she awoke early and lit the kerosene lamp beside her bed, put on her robe and slippers, and took the lamp with her to the kitchen. She put some kindling and a few sticks of wood in the cook stove to start a fire for her breakfast. After putting on a fresh pot of coffee, she went back to bathe and dress for her trip to town.

As she slipped on an apron, the coffee was through perking, and she prepared the rest of her breakfast. When she poured herself a cup of coffee, the loneliness seemed to envelop her. There was just no pleasure in sitting down to eat without someone to share it with.

After her chores, she took off her apron, hung it on a hook, picked up her shawl and purse off the bed, and left for town. She often stopped to talk on the way with strangers, townspeople that were outside working in their yards, or just her next-door neighbors. It was a small town, and everyone knew everybody else.

By the time she got through visiting, it was almost lunchtime. She was glad, because it was a treat to buy a hot dog at the counter of the five-and-dime store. She could smell those hot dogs as soon as she walked in the door, and they tasted as good as they smelled. Also there was always someone she knew that would sit down on the stool next to her and start a conversation.

Sure enough, she ran into Sister Elvira from church, and they enjoyed their chance encounter and hot dogs together. They talked about the new minister and his family and then caught each other up on their children and grandchildren. When they felt they had sufficiently filled each other in on the latest news, they said good-bye and went their separate ways.

Before she left, she went over to the fabric counter. They still had the pretty material she wanted, so she bought three yards. It was prettier than she remembered and decided it would make a nice frock for church. She left and started walking home and remembered the collard greens that Poss had brought her, so she stopped at the grocery store for some ham hock and cracklings.

When she got home, she felt very tired from her trip. Since it would take too long to cook the collards, she put off cooking them until the next day. She put the hocks and cracklings in the icebox.

She took her material back to the bedroom and put it away for a later time. After putting on her comfortable house slippers, she went to the front porch to rock for a while.

She was thinking again about the holidays and all the gifts she wanted to buy but could not afford. It was hard to make ends meet. She had memories of better times when she didn't have to worry about money, although they never had much in the way of material things. She remembered standing at the kitchen window and watching as her children played and how her pulse would skip a beat when she saw her husband walking briskly up the garden path toward home.

She tried to swallow a lump in her throat, and as it tightened, she choked back tears. She never allowed time for the luxury of feeling sorry for herself, but since all the children had moved away, she'd had too much time to think.

About then, she got up and walked back to the kitchen and decided she would have a light supper and go to bed early so she could read her Bible until she got sleepy. She wondered again why she was so tired and why it seemed the night, with the terrible loneliness that came with it, had a way of coming earlier than ever. It was still early evening and already turning as dark as night.

Just then, she heard a familiar whistle from out of the past coming up the garden path and saw someone walking briskly across the porch to the kitchen door.

Moments later, a couple strolled hand in hand down the garden path. They had a luminescence about them and wore raiment so magnificent it put even Sister Bessie in all her finery to shame. The woman's gown was of something that looked like gossamer with gold thread interwoven throughout the material.

The next day, in a sunny corner of the dining room, sat the empty rocking chair, and beside it was the much-used sewing basket with a faded and tattered dress stuffed inside. From down the hall came the sounds of muffled sobs while the scent of many flowers filled the air...

Epilogue

These contained works are both inert and extant in origin, and were created as an expression of healing through faith. While these passages reflect simpler times during which life's ebb, flow, and wane were woven within the fabric of family, the inevitabilities of life remain the same. It is my fervent hope that through these joyful introspections you may fully embrace your woe alongside the fortuitous strength instilled by life and loss.

~ Son of Author ~

www.ingramcontent.com/pod-product-compliance
Ingram Content Group UK Ltd.
Pitfield, Milton Keynes, MK11 3LW, UK
UKHW041930190726
13854UKWH00004B/1540